# A Day at the Petting Zoo

DK | Penguin Random House

### FIRST EDITION
**Series Editor** Deborah Lock, Penny Smith; **Art Editor** Jacqueline Gooden;
**US Editors** Elizabeth Hester, John Searcy; **Production** Alison Lenane; **DTP Designer** Almudena Díaz;
**Jacket Designer** Hedi Gutt; **Reading Consultant** Linda Gambrell, PhD

### THIS EDITION
**Editorial Management** by Oriel Square
**Produced for DK** by WonderLab Group LLC
Jennifer Emmett, Erica Green, Kate Hale, *Founders*

**Editors** Grace Hill Smith, Libby Romero, Michaela Weglinski;
**Photography Editors** Kelley Miller, Annette Kiesow, Nicole DiMella;
**Managing Editor** Rachel Houghton; **Designers** Project Design Company;
**Researcher** Michelle Harris; **Copy Editor** Lori Merritt; **Indexer** Connie Binder; **Proofreader** Larry Shea;
**Reading Specialist** Dr. Jennifer Albro; **Curriculum Specialist** Elaine Larson

**Published in the United States by DK Publishing**
1745 Broadway, 20th Floor, New York, NY 10019

Copyright © 2023 Dorling Kindersley Limited
DK, a Division of Penguin Random House LLC
23 24 25 26 27  10 9 8 7 6 5 4 3 2 1
001–333449–Apr/2023

A catalog record for this book
is available from the Library of Congress.
HC ISBN: 978-0-7440-6769-9
PB ISBN: 978-0-7440-6770-5

DK books are available at special discounts when purchased
in bulk for sales promotions, premiums, fundraising, or
educational use. For details, contact: DK Publishing Special Markets,
1745 Broadway, 20th Floor, New York, NY 10019
SpecialSales@dk.com

Printed and bound in China

The publisher would like to thank the following for their kind permission to reproduce their images:
a=above; c=center; b=below; l=left; r=right; t=top; b/g=background
**Dreamstime.com:** Adogslifephoto 8bl; **Fotolia:** Anatolii 13br; **Shutterstock.com:** Blur Life 1975 16c, narikan 15c,
Hayk_Shalunts 26c, shupian 30, Studio 11 20c
Cover images: *Front:* **Dreamstime.com:** Blue Ring Education Pte Ltd (grass), Arif Budiyana (clouds),
Evgenii Naumov (fences); **Shutterstock.com:** Rita_Kochmarjova b; *Back:* **Dreamstime.com:** Gunel Abbasova clb,
Colorfuelstudio cra, Pavel Naumov cla; *Spine:* **Shutterstock.com:** Rita_Kochmarjova
All other images © Dorling Kindersley

## For the curious
**www.dk.com**

# A Day at the Petting Zoo

We are at the
petting zoo.

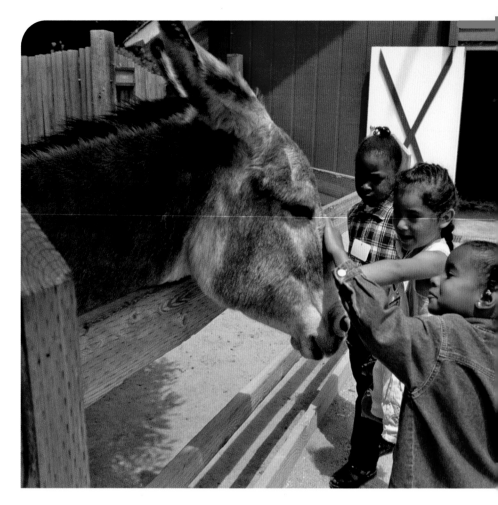

We are petting
a donkey.

**donkeys**

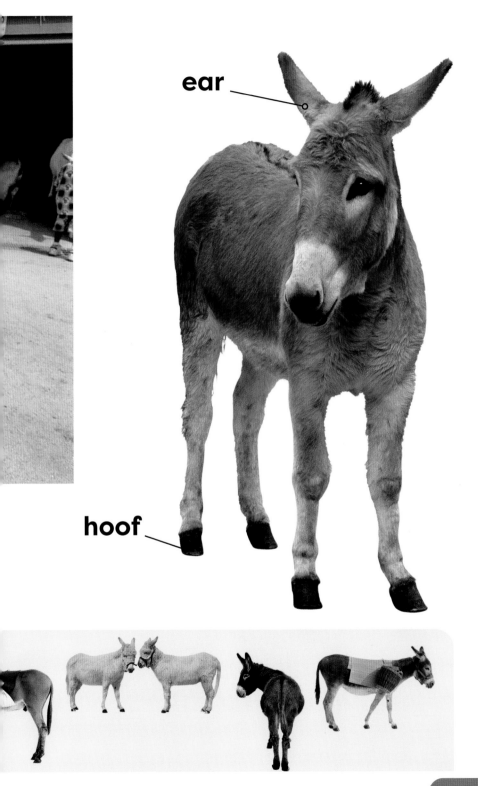

**ear**

**hoof**

# We are walking two baby llamas.

llamas

**leash**

I am brushing a pony.

**ponies and horses**

**mane**

**pigs and piglets**

I am picking up
a little
pink piglet.

snout

hoof

hen

**chicks**

I am holding
a soft yellow chick.

chick

I am carrying
a green stick insect.

**stick insects**

leaf

stick insect

**frogs**

# I am watching a beady-eyed frog.

Ribbit! Ribbit!

toe

It is mealtime now.
I am giving the
woolly lamb some milk.

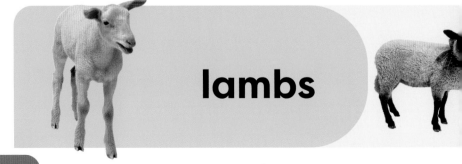

**lambs**

**wool**

**rabbits**

I am feeding
a hungry rabbit.

**ear**

**carrot**

This fluffy guinea pig
is eating a leaf.

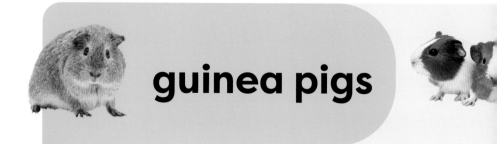

**guinea pigs**

**whiskers**

**claws**

# The white goose
# wants a snack.

**geese**

**feathers**

**bill**

**goats**

This long-horned goat is eating his lunch.

_____ **horn**

# Goodbye, animals!
It is time to go home.

# Glossary

**donkey**
a small horse-like animal with long ears

**frog**
a short animal with long back legs

**goose**
a large bird with a long neck and a bill

**llama**
a large, woolly animal from South America

**stick insect**
a long, thin insect that looks like a stick

# Quiz

Answer the questions to see what you have learned. Check your answers with an adult.

Which animal am I?

1. I am a fluffy animal with a long neck and pointed ears.

2. I am a pink animal with hooves and a snout.

3. I am a woolly baby sheep.

4. I am a bird with a long neck and a bill.

5. I have long horns and big, floppy ears.

1. A llama  2. A pig  3. A lamb  4. A goose  5. A long-horned goat